WAITING WOMEN

D1312933

WAITING WOMEN

first published by SPIKE PRESS in 1989

Reprinted in 1990, 1992, 1993, 1994 (twice) 1995, 1996

Revised Edition: 1999, 2002, 2005, 2009.

Copyright © Pauline Prior-Pitt 1999

www.pauline-prior-pitt.com

Publisher:
SPIKE PRESS, 112 Broomfield Road, Coventry CV5 6JZ

Distributor:
AVANTI BOOKS Unit 9, The io Centre, Whittle Way,
                    Arlington Business Park, Stevenage SG1 2BD

Printed and bound in Scotland by
Thomson Litho, 10/16 Colvilles Place, Kelvin Industrial Estate
East Kilbride, Glasgow G75 0SN

ISBN 1 872916 29 5

Pauline Prior-Pitt

WAITING WOMEN

SPIKE PRESS

Also by Pauline Prior-Pitt
further details at **www.pauline-prior-pitt.com**

Addresses & Dreams 1997
(Revised Edition 2004)

Storm Biscuits (2001)
Poems about the Island of North Uist

Ironing with Sue Lawley (2005)

Waiting Women CD (2003)
Live recording of selected poems

Pamphlets
These are hand made, hand stitched pamphlets, 15cms square.

North Uist Sea Poems (2005)
winner of the 2006 Callum Macdonald Award

Three Score Years & Some (2006)

Disappearing Out (2008)

ACKNOWLEDGEMENTS
Some of these poems first appeared in 'In the Heat of the
Moment', in 'Distaff', in 'Nutshell' and on Radio 4.

FOR

Martha, Jean, Charlotte, Annette, Phyllis

CONTENTS

Foreword by Maureen Lipman

The Angel	1
Choosing	2
Dancing Alone	3
The Dinner Party	4
The Girl He Fell in Love With	6
Talk	7
Waiting up	8
First Date	9
Language of Love	10
Moments	11
Cradle	12
Who Are You	13
"T" Shirts	14
Coming in from the Snow	15
Daughters	16
Family Tree	18
Supermarket Shopping	20
The Waste Bin	22
Well Actually I Do	23
The Empty House	24
One of These Days	25
Superwoman	26
Waiting Women	27
Calling All Women	28
Hot Flush	29
Cervical Smear	30
Women Should	31
The Obstetrician	32
Slipping	33

Just As	35
The Communal Changing Room	36
Men Don't Walk Fast Enough	38
Turning Out	40
In Her Rear View Mirror	41
Box of Chocolates	42
To Walk in the Dark Alone	44
Cracks	45
Blackbirds	46
End of Summer	47
Loreta	48
Encounter with a Pre-Raphaelite	49
Death in Hospital	50
White Cat	51
Goodbye	52
Last Night I Dreamed	54
No Rehearsal	55
Mountains	56
For a Friend	58

FOREWORD

Everyone needs a Pauline Prior-Pitt in their lives
and on their bookshelves. She reminds us to laugh
at ourselves, our foibles and our plans while still
praising the everlasting nature of love and constancy.

Her poetry is wry, accessible, and achingly funny.
There is scarcely a line I don't identify with.

Spread the word about Pauline Prior-Pitt.
                    She's an insurance against the blues.

MAUREEN LIPMAN

THE ANGEL

Be an Angel he said
make me a cup of tea.
She made it.

Be an Angel he said
iron a shirt for me.
She ironed it.

Be an Angel he said
listen to me.
She listened.

Be an Angel he said
let me do the talking
let me make decisions
let me choose.
She let him.

Be an Angel he said
make a home for me
bear my sons for me
always be there for me.
She was always there.

Be an Angel he said
lie beneath me
in the life I have made for you.

She turned away
and as he watched
she folded up her wings.

CHOOSING

A man does
what he chooses to do
first.

Then
if there's time
he does his chores.

A woman does
her chores
first.

Then...
there's never time
to do what she chooses.

DANCING ALONE

Last night I dreamed that you were with me still.
You stood before me wanting me to dance.
I seemed to know you were not there by chance
And once more I was subject to your will.

The music seemed so strange to me, but then
You showed me how to dance in step with you
So that we moved as one instead of two
And we performed a dance designed for men.

But then the music slowly changed its tone,
The strings began to play a different song.
It was my tune, and you did not belong.
I found a place where I could dance alone.

When I awoke it was as if I'd seen
Another life with you, caught in a dream.

THE DINNER PARTY

It should have been a most delightful evening,
Friends to dinner lovingly prepared.
The glasses shining softly in the lamplight,
The bottles open ready to be shared.

Gentle talk and laughter over sherry,
Holidays with white wine and the fish,
Children, jokes, a slight hint of aggression
During red wine and the main meat dish.

The host begins to be slightly offensive
To the guests that he's invited home to dine.
His loosened tongue and earthy conversation
Accompanies the pudding and sweet wine.

Abuse is hurled at one particular person.
A female guest is amorously kissed.
By the time the cheese and brandy's on the table
It is obvious that he's completely pissed.

He offers his insufferable opinions
And refuses to let other people speak,
Shouting at the hostess very loudly
When she tries to intervene and make the peace.

Strong black coffee doesn't help the situation,
He goes on talking louder than before
And pours himself another double brandy
Before sliding very slowly to the floor.

The guests feel that they should be going home now
And say how much they have enjoyed it all.
Saying that the food was most delicious
As they gather their belongings in the hall.

The door slams on the empty street at midnight.
The hostess and the host remain, alone.
It is time to rake up all those unhealed quarrels.
The worst part of the evening is to come.

THE GIRL HE FELL IN LOVE WITH

The girl he fell in love with
was bright and clever and gay.
She accepted his proposal
so he married her one day.

Married man has expectations.
He needs his wife to learn
to clean his house and cook his meals
and welcome his return.

Married man gets what he wants.
Wife stays at home indoors.
She cleans his house and cooks his meals,
does all the boring chores.

But boring chores make boring wives,
the man no longer sees
the girl so clever bright and gay
that used to fill his dreams.

The girl that he had married
to spend life pleasing him
has lost her own identity
responding to his whim.

The girl he left his wife for
was bright and clever and gay.
She accepted his proposal
so one day he moved away.

TALK

he talked
she listened

he talked
about himself

she listened to him
talking about himself

he talked until
he satisfied himself

she listened to
his satisfaction

she
could not speak

his ears were waxed
with self

she sat
silently tasting
the blood from her bitten lips

WAITING UP

It's past midnight
You're still out.
My mind is already widowed.
The police have been.
I've identified your body,
Chosen the hymns,
Comforted the children,
Sold your car to pay the bills,
Let the spare room.

Your key in the door.
"Sorry I'm late dear."

I could cheerfully kill you.

FIRST DATE

me   late for lunch
you   angry
me   sorry
you   forgiving
us   talking laughing
          eating drinking
          down the afternoon

time to go

you   to the theatre
me   to my flat
          part of the journey shared
          crushed together in the underground
we   rattle to your station

time to part

me   desperate
          to meet again
          aching for a farewell kiss

you
say   will you come to lunch
          with me again
          tomorrow
          then
          you kiss me
          disappearing
          from the train

THE LANGUAGE OF LOVE

Darling
Dearest
Sweetheart
Oodles
Boodles
Turtle dove.

It will not do.
Love has need of stronger language.
Hear me.

Hard words I have
Telling of needs
Of how I am.

Hurtful words
Of how you are not.

Let us not waste years
Each hiding self
in silences.

Let us speak
The language of love.

MOMENTS

If I could choose three moments,
I would choose
Walking in wellingtons
On wet sand
Holding your hand.

If I could choose two moments,
I would choose
In the kitchen, late at night
Both slightly tight
Putting our world right.

If I could choose one moment,
I would choose
In bed, you at my back
Enfolding me
Holding me.

CRADLE

The cradle stood empty
awaiting your presence.

I placed a hot bottle
between the small sheets
warming a place for you,

knowing in pain
you were ready.
The time had come
for your journey.

I remember the agony.
I remember your final
leap from my womb
as you fell into the sunlight.

And I remember
the last moment of my girlhood
when I warmed your cradle.

WHO ARE YOU

Who are you, child of my womb?
Such power you hold I have not known before.

Reverently I worship and adore you.
I bow down low to kiss your soft cheek.

Silently I listen for your breath.
Tenderly I hold and suckle you.

Your loving trap possesses and controls me.
Your crying times my days.

On dark days your screaming gnaws my brain.
My adoration is spurned. Your power overwhelms.

"T" SHIRTS

I'm going to get a "T" shirt
printed "PARENTS ARE OK".
It will be in lurid colours
and I'll wear it every day.

I'll buy another "T" shirt
printed "40 IS ALL RIGHT".
It will be in shiny purple
with the letters gold and white.
And I'll wear it when my children
bring their friends home late at night.

I'll buy another "T" shirt
printed "MOTHERS ARE THE BEST".
The words will be in lurex
stretching tight across my breast.
And I'll wear it when the children
would like me to look my best.

COMING IN FROM THE SNOW

When I came in from the snow,
across the park out of town,
you stared at me
standing:
blue wellies
green parka
red woolly hat.
You stared at
my carrier bag
HMV Records.

You've never been into HMV
looking like that.
You might have been seen
by one of my friends.

And I was with you,
black crombie
Doc Martens
close shaved head.
I walked beside your jeans, more holes than patches.
At your grandfather's 70th birthday party
for all the relations,
I danced with you.
And your feather earring.

So I was glad you were there
when I came in from the snow.

DAUGHTERS

What becomes of daughters
Nurtured in feminism
Bathed in equality
Independent
In charge
Daughters
With minds
Of their
Own

Daughters in love
Change
Independence
Disappears
No moves
Are made
Without
Consulting
Him

Daughter in love
Submerge
Go blindly
Hand in hand
Where
He
Wants
To
Go

Daughters in love
Forget
Their plans
Their futures
Trapped
Into
Pleasing
Only
Him

Oh Daughters
Wait
Don't lose yourselves
At twenty
To awaken
At forty
To wonder
Who
You
Are

FAMILY TREE

In Harrods window, trees created,
gold and red, sophisticated,
to perfection, decorated.

New shining baubles for our tree,
gold and red, I could just see
how beautiful our tree would be.

Now here it stands, my creation.
decorated to perfection,
the ideal Christmas colour scheme,
red and gold on darkest green.

Then they came in and made a fuss.
They didn't like it. It wasn't 'us'.

Where was the angel with the wobbly head
that Charlotte made in nursery school?
You can't leave her off the top, they said.

They brought down the box from under our bed.
Here's Paul's Father Christmas made of toilet rolls.
He usually goes about here, they said.

Then Adam found his Holy Ghost.
I think he really means 'Heavenly Host'.
It's a cardboard cross in silver and red.
I'll put it right at the front, he said.

Then I looked into the box and found
my man in the moon with his face so round,
the yellow house, the silver bell,
the little blue bird, my pale pink shell.

We hung them all on the tree as well.

What had become of my perfect creation,
my Christmas tree of sophistication,
my colour scheme of gold and red?

It looks much better now, they said.

SUPERMARKET SHOPPING

You make your list, drive to the store.
Parking the car can be a bore.

Collect your trolley, start to fill it,
stop when you can't get any more in it.

Off the shelf into the trolley
wait in the queue, oh what folly.

Out of the trolley onto the belt,
into the bags; no one to help.

Bags in the trolley, pay the bill,
out to the car, the boot to fill.

Push the trolley back to the shop,
into the car, home you pop.

Out of the boot, through the door,
can your arms take much more.

Into the cupboards, all put away,
carriers stowed for another day.

It makes me angry, it makes me shriek.
It'll all need doing again next week.

So I've been dreaming of a different plan.
It shouldn't be too hard for an intelligent woman.

This is what I'd like to do
to make my shopping dream come true.

I'll sit at my computer
call up my shopping list,

check with my store cupboard
to make sure nothing's missed.

I'll tap in every item.
Then wait a while until

I hear noises in the cupboard
as the shelves begin to fill.

The items that I've ordered
will arrive there on their own.

I'll have done the weekly shopping
without ever leaving home.

THE WASTE BIN

I must go down to the waste bin,
To the waste bin under the sink.
And all I ask is a clean bin,
One that doesn't stink

And all I ask is a neat bin
lined with a plastic sack,
To stop the gravy and fatty bits
From dripping down the back.

I must go and empty the waste bin,
The waste bin under the sink,
But what I'm going to find there
I really dread to think.

Oh our bin is crammed to the brim dears.
This really will have to stop,
Half eaten fish fingers, with custard
So carefully balanced on top.

The rubbish is crammed in so tightly
I can't get the bin liner out.
It splits as I try to remove it
And a lot of the custard falls out.

Oh I must go and empty the waste bin,
It's as full as full as can be.
But with four other waste bin users
Does it always have to be me?

WELL ACTUALLY I DO

Actually isn't really a poem word.
Really isn't a poem word actually.
Really doesn't actually mean much really.
However,
However isn't a poem word.
Really?

However,
I really need to use the word *actually* to say,
When it comes down to the basics of existence
Who **actually** puts the toilet roll on its holder
in your house?

THE EMPTY HOUSE

The house is quiet, still.
They've all gone out at last.
She wanders through each room

Picking up their droppings.
Folding and restoring them
Till all is calm and neat.

The hours ahead are hers.
Silence settles, soothing.
The empty rooms embrace.

She sits with her own thoughts,
Reads her book and falls asleep,
Wasting her solitude in dreams.

ONE OF THE DAYS

One of these days I'll just walk out
Leave you all
Go somewhere quiet
where I can be alone.

A whole night's sleep
Lunch in town
Read all afternoon
Where any mess is mine.

One of these days I'll just walk out
But not today
The baby isn't well
The fridge is nearly empty

There aren't any clean clothes
Then it's your birthday
And your mother's coming here for lunch on Sunday

One of these days...

SUPERWOMAN

Hi there!
This is superwoman

Slipping between cool sheets
To take part in the last act of the daily circus.

I've starred in every scene.
What a performance.

Principal cook
Leading Cleaner
Star laundress
Top of the bill chauffeur
Award winning mother.

So here comes the finale,
The climax is the sex act.

A round of applause please!

WAITING WOMEN

Women are all over, waiting.
Waiting for dating,
Waiting for mating,
Lying in waiting,
Awaiting gestating.

CALLING ALL WOMEN

This weekend
let's bend
the rules
and spend
the hours
pretending
we're the stronger sex.

Let's cruise
the motorways
in twos
searching out
the stranded
lone male
motorist.

Let's pretend
to be his friend
to lend
a hand
to mend...

or menace
for revenge.

HOT FLUSH

I'm in Tesco's
by the bread

when the heat
begins to spread

from my feet
up to my head

on fire
perspire

I'm wet
with sweat

Oh no not yet
just let

me get
out there

fresh air
or tear off shirt

stand here in underwear
or bare

then blush
hot flush

CERVICAL SMEAR

"Second door on the left.
Slip off your clothes below the waist,
including your knickers.
Wait for the nurse."

One cubicle, very small,
one door where she came in
one locked door opposite.
She slips off her clothes below the waist,
including her knickers
and waits.
And waits.

The locked door opens.
Another cubicle, very small
with curtains and a bed.

"Hop up on the bed dear
and wait for the doctor."
She hops up onto paper sheets
and waits
And waits.

"Bend your knees up
open your legs wide."
One knee rests gently
against the wall.
The other is left to flop.

The gloved hand approaches
bearing the speculum,
its duck bill shape
nearing that private place
of secret sexuality.

Unfamiliar violation of cold steel
jacked up
held open
light in position
shining on parts
felt, not seen by her.

Scrape round the cervix,
cells into the test tube,
let down the jack,
withdraw the duck's bill.
"You can get dressed now dear."

She returns to her clothes,
dresses below the waist,
including her knickers.

She wonders if the doctor knew her name.

WOMEN SHOULD STAY AT HOME TO LOOK AFTER THE CHILDREN

women should

women stay

women look after

after men

after children

after houses

should clean

should cook

should wash

stay ready

stay still

stay silent

THE OBSTETRICIAN

I would like to make a
constipated obstetrician
lie flat on his back
exposed in his shirt.
I would bend up his knees
and say , "Push!
Come on, bear down, push."

And when he said,
"Wouldn't squatting be more natural?"
I would ruffle his hair,
tell him to be a good boy,
smile a superior smile and say,
"Hush, we know best.
Now come along,
push, push,
push out all this bullshitting."

SLIPPING

Slipping
so easily
from
daughter
to
wife
to
mother
she
wondered
who
she
would
be
if
ever
she
had
the
chance
to
be
herself.

JUST AS

Just as
the young people
leave,
leasing me
back to myself
again

freeing spaces
outside
and in,
the old people
begin

to occupy
my edges
and I fall
back
into the loving trap.

THE COMMUNAL CHANGING ROOM

The changing room is over there
The assistant says with a vacant stare.
It's over in the corner dear.
I approach with mounting fear.
Pull back the curtain, peer within.
Oh my goodness, all that bare skin.

Beautiful women, bodies so slim
stare at me as I creep in.
Youthful girls with slender thighs
try on clothes not made in my size.
They stand near naked for all to see,
not hiding in the corner like me.

But I've got money to spend
so I try to pretend
that I couldn't care less.
I start to undress.
I look such a mess.

Just look at my bum.
The colour's too bright.
I look such a sight.
Well the top is alright
but the bottom is tight.

From the corner of my eye I see
Youthful glances inspecting me,
Turn quickly away and smile at each other,

She's old enough to be my mother.
Who is she kidding? What is she at?
She's far too old and far too fat.

I dress with haste.
Not to my taste.
Too big round the waist.
Need I say more to the girl at the door

I wander along to where I belong.
To look for a dress
from M&S.

MEN DON'T WALK FAST ENOUGH

If you're shopping for clothes
leave the men at home.
Men don't walk fast enough,
keep stopping outside camera shops.

They lack focus, go wandering off
into other departments, don't
come back to where they were
and you waste time searching for them.
They never search for you.

Men are so logical.
They expect you to buy the first dress you try.
You like it, it suits you, buy it!
You try to explain that this is only a 'maybe' dress.
A 'maybe, at the end of the day
when you've been into every other shop
and haven't found anything better,
you may come back and try it on again' dress.

How can you possibly know
until you've been into every shop
tracking down the rails
that there won't be something better
in a size, shape, and colour,
that makes you look slimmer, and younger.

You can't blame them, most of them
don't even shop for their own clothes.
Their wives know the kind of thing they wear.

They carry their collar, chest, waist
and inside leg length in their heads.
Provide a made to measure
'take away' service from M&S.
Well you can always take it back.

Men don't want to make a day of it.
They wait outside the changing rooms
in such a way that makes you rush
and you can't make up your mind.

Then they say, "Take your time.
I'll just pop into Waterstones while you decide.
See you outside in ten minutes."

You wait outside for him and after for ever
he arrives with a pile of books
saying he's been waiting all this time
and surely you bought that dress.

He needs to be told that,
if you know exactly what you're looking for before you start,
you won't find anything.
And if you don't know what you're looking for,
you've an open mind, you might find something.

But if you go home with nothing,
you'll have tried things on and know what to look for next time.
When you'll be leaving him at home
and going on your own.

TURNING OUT

This Laura Ashley dress will have to go.
You know the sort I mean, fashionable in the 70s.
This one's in needlecord, a subtle aubergine
with small blue spots and holly leaves.

We all wore them before power dressing came about.
It's too romantic now. I'll have to throw it out.

It suits me almost to the ground,
a gently fitting bodice, covered buttons to the waist,
two pockets in the softly gathered skirt
and long leg o'mutton sleeves with buttoned cuffs.

The leg o'mutton sleeves could be undone,
cut out again to give a softer line.
The gathers in the skirt could be refined.
I could dye the whole thing black. I'll put it back.

I said that last time. And the time before.
But for now, I'll slip it back into the drawer
with the torn silk shirt I'm going to mend,
the Jaeger suit, still too small,
and the mohair cardigan, fawn, never worn.

And if it's in there next time when I'm turning out,
then I'll almost definitely throw it out.

IN HER REAR VIEW MIRROR

In her rear view mirror
a silver Jaguar.
She levels her eyes
on a dark handsome male.

A left turn, he follows.
A twisting country lane,
he is close behind.
Her taught body softens.

Cello strings are yearning
the Elgar concerto.
Warm sun through the window.
Fields of ripening corn.

At the narrow crossroads
she plunges straight over.
In her rear view mirror
only overhanging leaves.

THE BOX OF CHOCOLATES

The box of chocolates that you sent,
I know that it was kindly meant
But to resist requires a lot
Of willpower, which I haven't got.

Safely wrapped in cellophane
And hidden on the highest shelf
A box is safe for several days,
Until I have to tempt myself.

Once the cellophane's undone
I tell myself I'll just have one.
But one alone is not enough
I catch the taste and start to stuff.

Chocolate fudge, montelimar,
Hard centres, but my favourites are
The caramel and creamy coffee,
Hazel nut and liquid toffee.

The strawberry creams are not for me
They're far too sweet and sickly
But when they're the only ones left in the box
Even they disappear very quickly.

I know that carrot sticks are crunchy.
That celery is very munchy.
Radishes are tasty too
But chocolate is bad for you.

So next time when you want to say,
Thank you for a lovely day,
Please can you think of something that
Won't add to all my layers of fat.

A book, some scent, a bottle of wine
Or a bunch of flowers would be just fine.

TO WALK IN THE DARK ALONE

To walk in the dark alone,
To walk without fear.

No quickening of pulse
Through the subway.

No quickening of pace
Between street lamps.

To cross the park serene.
To pass the stranger with a smile.

CRACKS

Such beautiful wallpaper
a perfect covering for cracks in the plaster
finer than spiders webs.

Such a beautiful couple
a perfect relationship
carefully papered by smiles.

Peeling wallpaper reveals
plaster shattered like dropped pastry
exposing structural damage.

BLACKBIRDS

Two blackbirds courted in delight
Within my town house garden walls.
Follow my leader dawn to dusk,
His sweet song echoed by her calls.

She flutters, he flutters.
She hops, he hops.
A swoop, a swoop,
A scuttle, a scuttle,
A short flight, a short flight.
He preens, displaying his physique,
his glossy coat, his golden beak.

But yesterday he came alone.
He sang and sang,
She did not come.

Has she flown off, the flighty piece
to build a nest with some bird else?
Is she in some deep disgrace
to keep her from her favoured place?
Or is she lying dead, alone,
Far from him. And cannot come?

Today his dusty feathers fall.
He calls no more upon the wall
He simply stands with yellow gape
Mourning the absence of his mate.

END OF SUMMER

The sun no longer brightens bedrooms early.
Night comes too soon, dulling summer's easy spirit.
Hot afternoons catch us out in wool sweaters
Worn to protect us from cold mornings.

The house martens have long since flown
And geese are now practising formations
Honking instructions, as leader supersedes
leader in their long skeined flight.

Leaves that only recently uncurled
And shaded us, loose their hold and fall.
Ahead dull days and dark hours
Wait to welcome winter.

LORETA aged 24
(died Vilnius, Saturday 12 January 1991)

On the dark hillside the people are waiting,
Defending the huge concrete media tower,
Transmitting their plight to the rest of the world.

Alone by her campfire Loretta is praying.
Into the darkness she hears tanks approaching.
In bitter cold she prays for her land.

The soviet tanks are climbing the hillside,
Advancing relentlessly, tearing a track way,
ploughing through hedges and tearing the ground.

As they loom nearer, one pauses, rolls backwards.
Loreta runs shouting, "You fascists!   Lithuania!"
A few fractured flowers wave in her hand.

The tank shifting forward, lunges towards her,
Crushing her young body into the ground.

The flowers she carries fly up before her,
Falling to rest in the eye of the tank.

ENCOUNTER WITH A PRE-RAPHAELITE

From her portrait, dark tresses tumbling,
one arm resting on marble,
this slender maiden beckons

and I walk towards her, smiling
in that carefree way I have with smiles,
marvelling at the silken folds, the skin tones,

the way her eyes encounter mine,
without warning, seeming to say,
death is forever and ever.

And I am back in the black space
strangling the screams in my throat
as, in the silence of the gallery

I whisper my rehearsed lines to her.
"It's not the dying, it's the not being,
no me on earth, all going on without me,

forever and ever, dead. Is it only me?"
"No" replies the damsel in the landscape,
"I am screaming too."

DEATH IN HOSPITAL

Death images:
curtains, a darkened room, silence.

So why is she here in this bright ward
haunted by old girls calling confusion,
Coronation Street on in the corner,

where urine stains the air
and sheets are changed by brisk blue nurses
running out of time.

Not the death she had imagined,
as slowly, slowly,
in full view
she sucks in her last breath
her last breath.

WHITE CAT

White cat lying on a wall
stretched out in the sun
undisturbed by barking dogs
not moving, not living,
stretched out, dead.

My mother lying on her bed
her young body still warm
stretched out, not moving
gone from me.

My father lying on white sheets
his body so small
that was my protector
stretched out, not moving.
Mine was not the hand he loosed in death.

White cat, lying on a wall,
your death looked so unchallenging.

GOODBYE
for Martha

and did you know
that this

would be
your Deathday

you had not been told
how ill

you were not
involved

it was not
happening

we were to
keep it from you

pretending
as always

and were you
keeping it

did you long to cry out
I'm dying
yet say nothing

you must have known

and did you wonder
how we'd be without you

and did you feel afraid
and couldn't say

and did you long to hold
to hold us to you

and say
goodbye

goodbye

LAST NIGHT I DREAMED

Last night I dreamed that you were with me still
And lay beside me in our marriage bed.
You smiled at me and gently stroked my head,
Familiar gesture rousing me until

The sunlight touched the curtain, making gold
To spill across the covers of our bed.
And turning to me jokingly you said,
I'll always love you, even when you're old.

You laughed and tickled me and I replied
That I would never be as old as you.
But in the dream I knew this wasn't true
And as my body welcomed yours I cried.

When I awoke you were not in your place
And silent grieving tears covered my face.

NO REHEARSAL

No rehearsal this, for other lives,
with life, like parts prepared, and our mistakes
cancelled out to start again. Oh no!

This is your only chance, so choose with care
and treasure every age. For soon your time
upon the stage will cease and you will be

as dead as ashes after burning leaves.
Your eternity will lie with friends
and small resemblances in future kin

not in some unfound heaven up above.
Life will go on without you. You have had
your turn. No action replays are allowed.

So scream your silent death fears if you must.
Your final part will be as of the dust.

MOUNTAINS

Did we have to climb
to the top of every mountain
crawling on all fours
shouting into the wind

You said
the view
would be
magnificent

On sunny days it was
but often it was cloud swept
and we saw nothing
except our two selves exposed

Other couples
were striding out on lower paths
skirting the mountain
yet still arriving

Did we have to climb
to the top of every mountain
only to plunge
into deeper and deeper valleys

You in your stout boots
me barefoot dressed
for dancing in the waves
at the sea's edge

Yes we had to climb
to the top of every mountain
lifting the layers of rock

leaving behind the stones and grit
till scarcely a thin film
of dust remained

Yes we had to plunge
into the valleys
to clothe ourselves in leaves

from the same tree
to walk for a while
on soft grass

When the skin
on my feet
has grown hard

we will cross
the pebbled shore
sharp with shells

we will wade
in the water
and laugh at the mountains

and we will dance
at the sea's edge
in the evening tide

FOR A FRIEND

You say the test
was positive
and ask for a poem.

Positive.
Your decorated eyes
shocked wide
with held back tears.

Positive.
Your sexy voice
A lump in your breast
malignant.

and your fear
catches me.
Positive you say
and ask for a poem.

There must be words
words to comfort
words to warm
to melt
to mop up
icy fear,

words to smooth
to soothe
the bruising
anger,

words to lighten
to brighten
often to soften,

words to bless
caress
enfold
and hold
and hold.

There must be words.